Designed by Flowerpot Press
www.FlowerpotPress.com
CHC-0909-0474
ISBN: 978-1-4867-1651-7
Made in China/Fabriqué en Chine

Chemistry is a really fun science to understand, because it is all around us. Did you know doctors, nurses, veterinarians, engineers, chefs, and mad scientists all use chemistry? And they're not the only ones—everyone uses chemistry every day without even knowing it!

Chemistry is why food tastes so yummy and why magnets stick to things. It is why rain falls to the ground and it is even why rockets can blast up to the Moon! Chemistry is a really important part of the world around us.

Why do atoms seem invisible?
Are they just really good at playing hide-and-seek?

Atoms are the building blocks of life, the universe, and everything! You, the food you eat, the house you live in, the earth you live on, and even the stars and Moon in the sky are ALL made up of atoms. They are like real-life connector blocks. We can't see them individually because they are tiny, but when they get together, they make up everything we see.

An atom is made up of three things: protons, neutrons, and electrons. Protons are positively charged, electrons are negatively charged, and neutrons have no charge. The protons and neutrons hug together in the middle of an atom in what we call the nucleus. The electrons fly around them in orbits called the electron cloud. All these components come together in a wide variety of combinations to make up what we call the elements.

How do you tell elements apart if they are all just groups of atoms?

Do you ask each of them to wear different costumes?

Different costumes?!?! No way!

You can tell different elements from each other by the way they are structured. Even though atoms make up everything, everything doesn't look and act the exact same. For example, your brother doesn't look like a dog even though they're both made up of atoms. This is because not all atoms are the same.

You can have different types of atoms just like you can have different types of ice cream. If you add different amounts of ingredients (protons, neutrons, and electrons), you get different flavors. These different "flavors" of atoms are what we call elements. All the known elements make up what is called the Periodic Table of Elements which is like the menu at your favorite ice-cream shop.

How do molecules form groups?

Do they all meet in a singing competition?

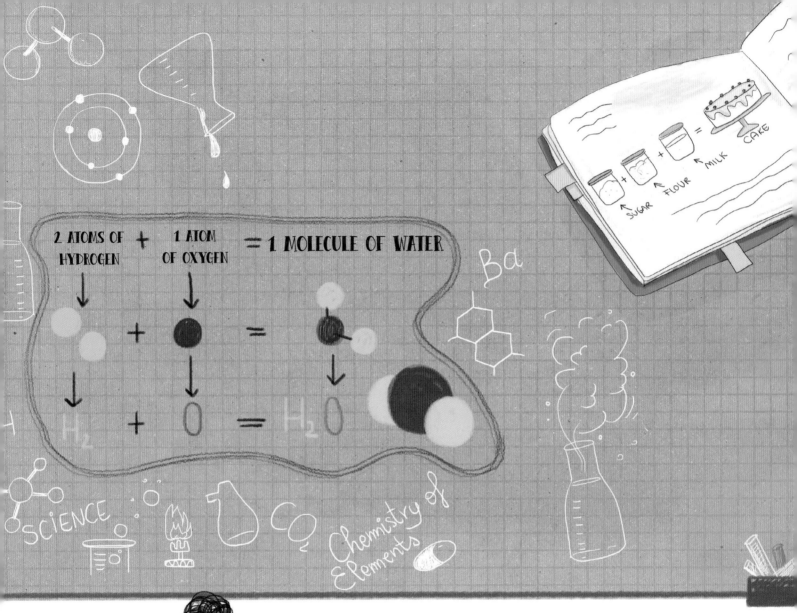

2 ATOMS OF HYDROGEN + 1 ATOM OF OXYGEN = 1 MOLECULE OF WATER

H_2 + O = H_2O

Ba

SCIENCE

CO_2

Chemistry of Elements

SUGAR + FLOUR + MILK = CAKE

A singing competition?!?! No way!

Elements are too small to do much on their own, so they typically form groups with other elements. We call these groups molecules. When the group is made up of more than one kind of element, the molecule can also be called a compound. Molecules tend to be the things we can actually see in the world, like water (made up of two hydrogen atoms and one oxygen atom: H_2O) or salt (made up of one sodium atom and one chlorine atom: NaCl). Similar to a recipe, molecules are made from specific amounts of different elements coming together to make something new. For a cake, you may need to add one cup of sugar, one cup of flour, and one cup of water, but for a molecule of water, you need two hydrogen atoms and one oxygen atom.

How do forces in chemistry interact?
Are they magical forces that play tricks on each other?

Magical forces?!?! No way!

The two main forces in chemistry are positive forces and negative forces.

Have you heard the saying "opposites attract"? It may not be true for everything, but it is true of forces.

PROTON
positive charge

ELECTRON
negative charge

attraction

repulsion

attraction

repulsion

A force can either be positive or negative. If two forces are opposite, meaning one is positive and one is negative, they attract each other and want to be close together. When two forces are the same, either both positive or both negative, they repel each other and want to be far apart.

Remember how protons are positive and electrons are negative? This is why atoms interact with each other so well and can form molecules. Some elements have a stronger positive effect while some have a stronger negative effect. This gets determined by the number of protons and electrons in an atom.

When strongly positive and strongly negative atoms are near each other, the positive force attracts the negative forces and pulls the electrons in closer. This forms bonds between the atoms and allows them to make bigger things like compounds and molecules.

hydrogen
H +

hydrogen
H +

8 −
8 +
oxygen

WATER = H₂O

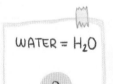

O

H   H

NEGATIVE FORCES

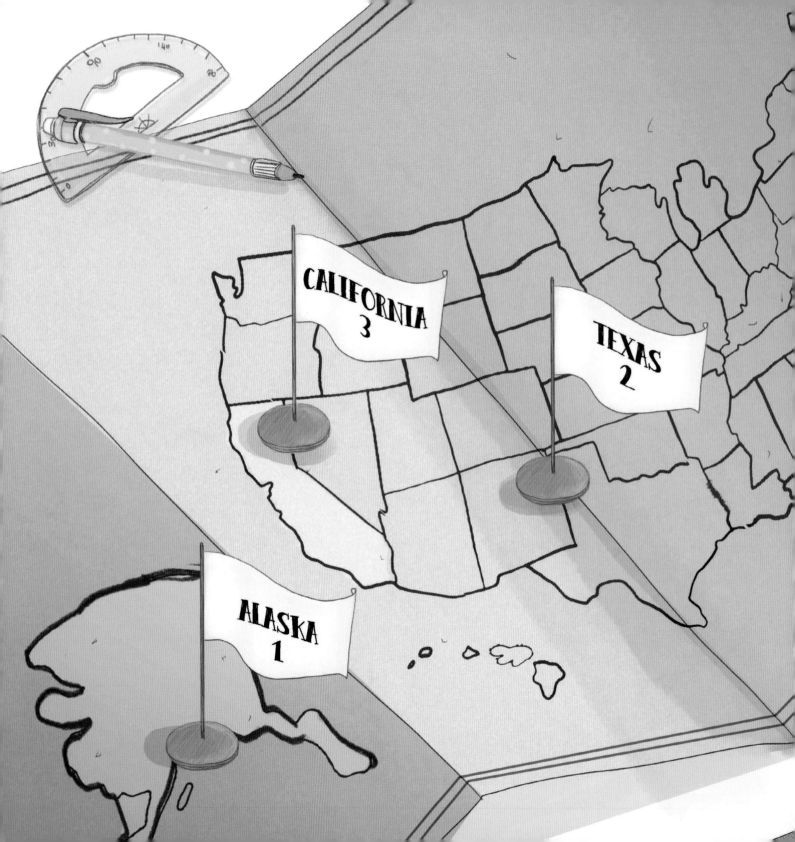

How do you know the three main states of matter?
Are they just the three biggest states in the
United States of America?

American states?!?! No way!

Anything physical, including any type of atom or compound, is collectively referred to as matter. There are three main states of matter: solid, liquid, and gas.

Solids are the state of matter in which atoms or molecules pack in really close to each other so there's not a lot of room to move around. Atoms in solids pack in tight so that they can't slide or move past each other, meaning they have a fixed shape. Solids are materials like wood, metal, and glass.

solid

liquid

Liquids are the state of matter in which atoms and molecules can slide past each other a little more easily than solids but still can't go too far. Liquids can also change their shape to fit the container they are in. Liquids are things like water, coffee, and juice.

SOUP

coffee

STATES OF MATTER

Gases are the most excited and energetic of the states of matter. Atoms in a gas have plenty of room between each other and can bounce around really fast. Gases can be compressed or expanded depending on how much space they have to move around. Like liquids, gases can change their shape to fit the container they are in. The air you breathe and the helium in balloons are both examples of gases.

gas

How do chemical reactions work?
Are they the same as human reactions?

Similar to human reactions, chemical reactions are the way different substances respond to each other.

Reactions are the rearranging of atoms and bonds to change from one set of substances to a different set of substances. The compounds that go into reactions are referred to as reactants. The compounds that come out of reactions are referred to as products. When a reaction occurs, the bonds in the reactants break, the atoms move around, and new bonds are formed to make new products. Sometimes reactions require heat or energy input to drive them. Other times heat or energy can be one of the products.

Enjoy!

Product!

let them cool!

This is the change in which the new substance is formed!

Bake!

A new bond is forming from heat input.

CHEMISTRY IN THE WORLD

Water is a great example of all of the states of matter and the ways they can change. If you have a glass of water with ice cubes, you have two states of matter. You have the liquid water you drink and the solid ice cubes. But what happens if you leave the glass of water out in the sun on a hot day?

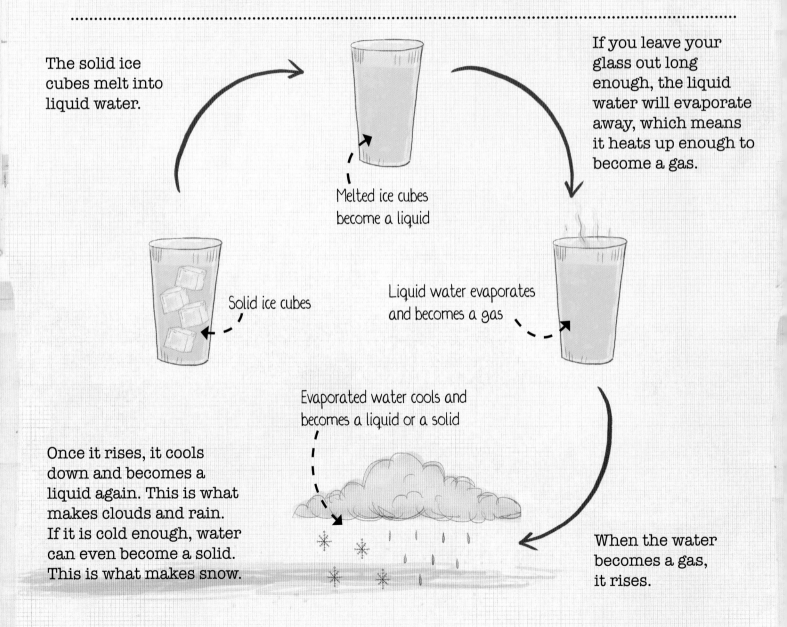

The solid ice cubes melt into liquid water.

Melted ice cubes become a liquid

If you leave your glass out long enough, the liquid water will evaporate away, which means it heats up enough to become a gas.

Solid ice cubes

Liquid water evaporates and becomes a gas

Evaporated water cools and becomes a liquid or a solid

Once it rises, it cools down and becomes a liquid again. This is what makes clouds and rain. If it is cold enough, water can even become a solid. This is what makes snow.

When the water becomes a gas, it rises.

THE STATES OF MATTER

As you learned on the previous page, matter can change from one state to another. Look at the examples below to see how states of matter can change in four different ways.

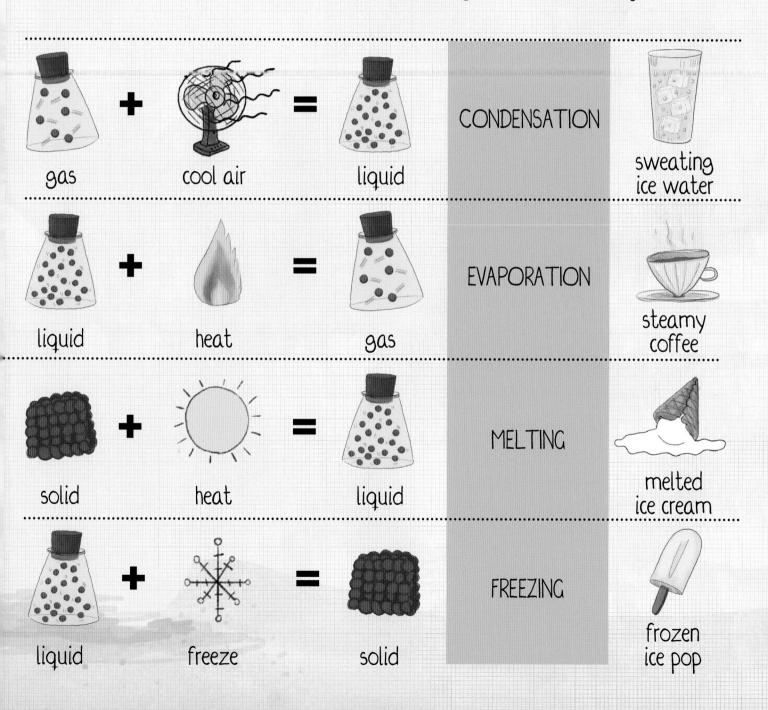

gas	cool air	liquid	CONDENSATION	sweating ice water
liquid	heat	gas	EVAPORATION	steamy coffee
solid	heat	liquid	MELTING	melted ice cream
liquid	freeze	solid	FREEZING	frozen ice pop

This is the Periodic Table of Elements. You can read the table using the green key below. Can you find some of the elements from the book?

Periodic Table

Hydrogen is the most abundant element in the universe.

The only letter that doesn't appear on the Periodic Table is J.

The rows of the Periodic Table are called periods.

The columns of the Periodic Table are called groups or families.

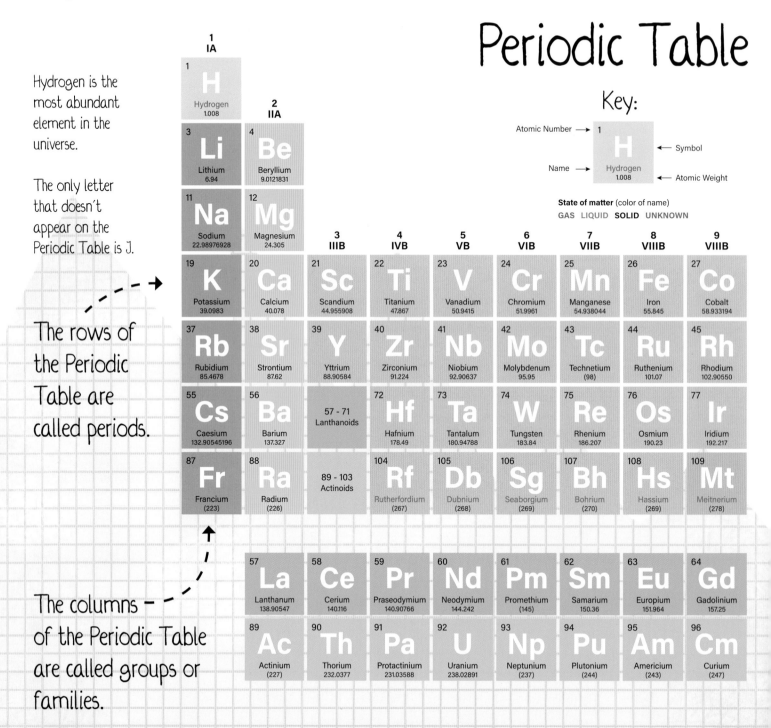

Can you find all of these elements below: oxygen, aluminum, helium, mercury, hydrogen, nitrogen, carbon, and chlorine?

# of Elements

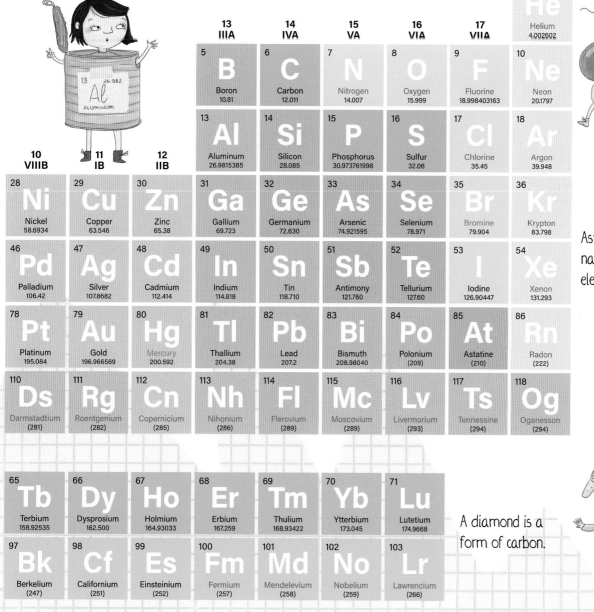

			18 VIIIA
			2 **He** Helium 4.002602

13 IIIA	14 IVA	15 VA	16 VIA	17 VIIA	
5 **B** Boron 10.81	6 **C** Carbon 12.011	7 **N** Nitrogen 14.007	8 **O** Oxygen 15.999	9 **F** Fluorine 18.998403163	10 **Ne** Neon 20.1797
13 **Al** Aluminum 26.9815385	14 **Si** Silicon 28.085	15 **P** Phosphorus 30.973761998	16 **S** Sulfur 32.06	17 **Cl** Chlorine 35.45	18 **Ar** Argon 39.948

10 VIIIB	11 IB	12 IIB						
28 **Ni** Nickel 58.6934	29 **Cu** Copper 63.546	30 **Zn** Zinc 65.38	31 **Ga** Gallium 69.723	32 **Ge** Germanium 72.630	33 **As** Arsenic 74.921595	34 **Se** Selenium 78.971	35 **Br** Bromine 79.904	36 **Kr** Krypton 83.798
46 **Pd** Palladium 106.42	47 **Ag** Silver 107.8682	48 **Cd** Cadmium 112.414	49 **In** Indium 114.818	50 **Sn** Tin 118.710	51 **Sb** Antimony 121.760	52 **Te** Tellurium 127.60	53 **I** Iodine 126.90447	54 **Xe** Xenon 131.293
78 **Pt** Platinum 195.084	79 **Au** Gold 196.966569	80 **Hg** Mercury 200.592	81 **Tl** Thallium 204.38	82 **Pb** Lead 207.2	83 **Bi** Bismuth 208.98040	84 **Po** Polonium (209)	85 **At** Astatine (210)	86 **Rn** Radon (222)
110 **Ds** Darmstadtium (281)	111 **Rg** Roentgenium (282)	112 **Cn** Copernicium (285)	113 **Nh** Nihonium (286)	114 **Fl** Flerovium (289)	115 **Mc** Moscovium (289)	116 **Lv** Livermorium (293)	117 **Ts** Tennessine (294)	118 **Og** Oganesson (294)

Astatine is the rarest naturally occurring element.

65 **Tb** Terbium 158.92535	66 **Dy** Dysprosium 162.500	67 **Ho** Holmium 164.93033	68 **Er** Erbium 167.259	69 **Tm** Thulium 168.93422	70 **Yb** Ytterbium 173.045	71 **Lu** Lutetium 174.9668
97 **Bk** Berkelium (247)	98 **Cf** Californium (251)	99 **Es** Einsteinium (252)	100 **Fm** Fermium (257)	101 **Md** Mendelevium (258)	102 **No** Nobelium (259)	103 **Lr** Lawrencium (266)

A diamond is a form of carbon.

GLOSSARY

Atoms – the building blocks of all elements that are made up of a nucleus and the surrounding electron cloud; they can be combined with other atoms to form molecules

Attract – to pull toward each other

Bond – a force that holds the atoms in a molecule together

Chemical Reaction – a change that occurs when substances come together to form new substances

Chemistry – a science that studies the structure and properties of substances and the changes they go through with each other

Compound – a substance that is created when the atoms of two or more elements join together

Compress – to squeeze together to become smaller

Electron – a very small particle of matter that has a negative charge of electricity; electrons travel around the outside of the nucleus of an atom in the electron cloud

Electron Cloud – the group of electrons surrounding the nucleus of an atom

Element – a substance made up of only one type of atom that can be identified by the specific number of protons, neutrons, and electrons it has

Expand – to increase in size or become bigger

Forces – something that causes interactions between atoms by either attraction or repulsion; they can be positive or negative forces

Gas – atoms that can freely bounce around and can change shape and volume to fit their container

Liquid – atoms that slide around each other and can change shape but not volume

Matter – anything that has mass or takes up space

Molecule – a substance that is created when two or more atoms join together

Negative Force – a force that attracts positive forces and repels other negative forces; electrons have a negative force

Neutron – a very small particle of matter that has no electrical charge; neutrons are part of the nucleus of an atom

Nucleus – the central part of an atom; it is made up of protons and neutrons

Periodic Table of Elements – a collective list of all the known chemical elements arranged according to their unique properties

Positive Force – a force that attracts negative forces and repels other positive forces; protons have a positive force

Product – a substance formed as a result of a chemical reaction

Proton – a very small particle of matter with a positive electrical charge; protons are part of the nucleus of an atom

Reactant – a substance that goes into a chemical reaction

Repel – to force away from each other

Solid – compact atoms that cannot change shape or volume

States of Matter – the forms in which matter can exist, typically as a gas, a liquid, or a solid

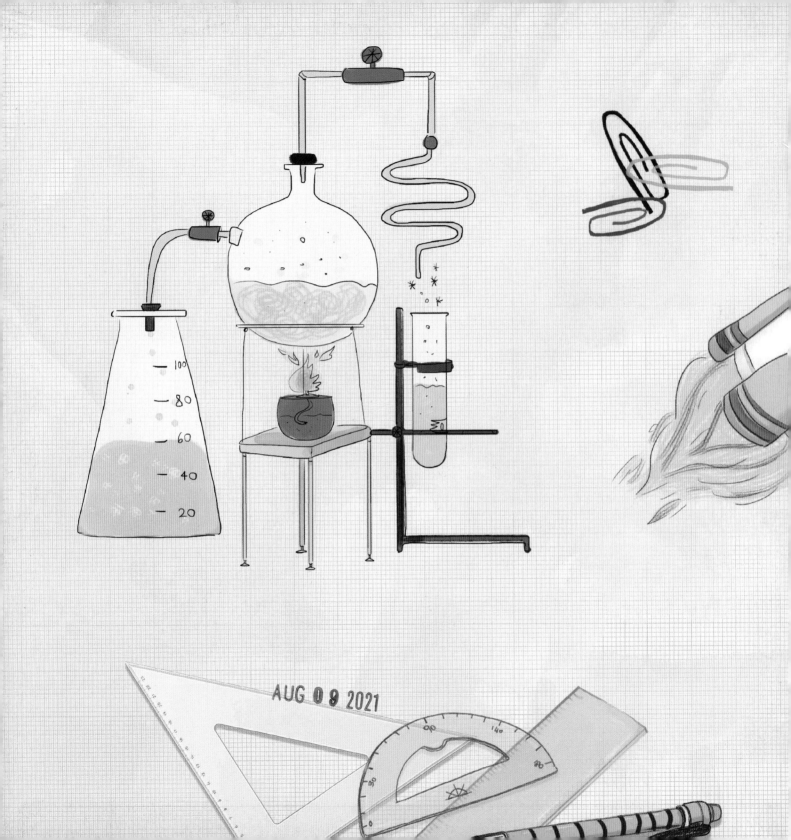

AUG 09 2021